POSTCARDS FROM TEXAS

Allyson Whipple

Postcards from Texas

©2023 Allyson Whipple
All Rights Reserved

First Printing

ISBN 978-1-7350257-7-3

CUTTLEFISH
BOOKS

ADVANCED PRAISE

In Postcards from Texas, each haiku stands on its own while also contributing to a subtle narrative of a unique individual experiencing the passage of time in a specific place. Allyson Whipple takes familiar objects from our human world (an air conditioner, trash cans), combines them with natural elements (a cicada, bluebonnets), and weaves them together with unobtrusive expressions of deep, complex, and universal emotions. Each rereading further reveals the generosity and thoughtfulness of these "postcards."

Warren Decker
author of *The Long Side of the Midnight Sun*

Allyson Whipple's first book of Japanese forms, Postcards from Texas, follows a goodbye year of astute observations of many of the typical Texas tropes—bluebonnets, oaks, cicadas, mockingbirds, grackles, prickly pears, sticker burrs—as well as things that aren't always associated with Texas—homeless people, rent increases, climate change, floodplains, condemned buildings. As another former Texan, I appreciate the specific details of both the good and bad of the Texas landscapes and towns/cities. These "postcards" are a strong reminder of the place we both left and of our similar trajectories into the world of haiku.

Scott Wiggerman
Co-Editor, *Lifting the Sky:*
Southwestern Haiku and Haiga

In these haiku of witness, Allyson Whipple has crafted an earnest love letter to Texas. Each of these fifty-three worshipful poems speaks towards the changing landscape of this humid, sprouting, gentrified, grackle-sung, deeply-loved state, practicing attention as devotion. With heat and love, she manages to hold the sorrow alongside the beauty. She pulls from the in-between spaces a long, sure heartroot: the "plastic rose [jutting] from a scarred oak," "rain lilies' sprouting 'around the demolition notice,' and 'century blossoms / tangled in power lines." In these pages, Whipple renders Texas' heartbreak alongside its steady swell of belonging, practicing the slow and careful work it takes to become devoted to place: "pulling sticker burrs / from pant legs / one by one."

Zoë Fay-Stindt
author of *Bird Body*

Being one of the hardest working, most dedicated and prolific movers and shakers in the international short form writing and critical community, it's particularly exciting news and a distinct delight to discover Allyson Whipple has collected her thrilling poetry and is releasing it to the fortunate public. Keen admirers of the stunning composition and dazzling perspectives of this author can well understand why these contents are of such enormous value to the English Language Haiku landscape and will be treasured and appreciated enthusiastically by literature lovers familiar and new alike — both as a source of rich, edifying pleasure and immersive sensorial storytelling, and as valuable tools for understanding the craft and mechanics of composing tight, impactful haiku and senryu poetry which stuns and enchants, moves and stirs the audience, and stays impressed upon contemplative minds long after encountering.

Postcards From Texas, in celebrating the resplendent natural world and its reflections and parallels in powerful human drama, provides a compelling testament to the singular voice and incisive pen of one of our day's most beguiling haijin. A micro poem is not unlike a missive, and Texas is an intriguing setting from which to receive gonzo reportage, particularly navigating these contentious times of ours we traverse on tiptoes, avoiding innumerable invisible landmines as species and nations. Drawing upon a unique perspective, with razor-sharp wit and striking concrete language, an impressive formal toolbox and range of interdisciplinary wisdom, unparalleled experience and eclectic grasp of (among many subjects) cuisine and its connections to poetry – gleaned hosting a beloved widely acclaimed podcast where her encyclopedic knowledge on the most diverse topics, rapid-fire recall is always evident and astonishing – Whipple has crafted an important and deeply personal collection here, which it behooves the international community to take note of and thoughtfully explore. Somewhere between love letter (from a refugee, to a place and time which no longer exists) and postcard from the edge, a nexus point between Eastern and Western aesthetics, faiths and ideologies, contrasting the global north and south, progress and conservatism, individual or collective, urban and rural, pagan and puritan, rapacious and environmental, idealist and jaded, old world and new, migrant and native, artificial and organic, these juxtapositions and the highly charged tension between each energize the subtexts, and each discrete piece within, providing the student much food for consideration to reflect thoughtfully upon at length.

Matsuo Basho once posited that "those who have no traveling experience along the Tokaido [the old inter-city highway] are quite unlikely to become good at poetry." True to the tradition of wandering spiritual hermitry (it's no coincidence nomadic birds and honeybees figure prominently as leitmotifs) in magnificent rapport with the elements and their relation to things temporal, in Allyson Whipple's *Postcards from Texas*, the exodus and its memorializing chronicled, we find much support for that argument and explanations for what has made this poet such a qualified and thrilling writer of short form excellence. It's also distinctive and noteworthy how masterfully Allyson applies the arts of wabi and sabi, carefully with deftness unearths the beauty in poverty, pain, loss, and melancholy scenes or vignettes, making us each appreciate what we have and had through considering declines and absences. Don't miss these cherries blossoming! The views are quite unforgettable and spectacular! These are poems you'll want to Xerox and tape up on your refrigerator or in your workplace! A remarkable feat to be sure, worth experiencing for yourself!

Jerome Berglund
editor, *Heterodox Haiku Journal*

DEDICATION

dedicated to
Devorah Winegarten,
Paul Whipple,
Wade Martin,
John DiPalma,
and Joe Bratcher III
in memoriam

ACKNOWLEDGEMENTS

Grateful appreciation is offered to the editors and publishers of *Akitsu Quarterly, Autumn Moon, bottle rockets, Cold Moon Journal, #FemkuMag, Haiku Dialogue, Miriam's Well, Poetry Pea, Texas Poetry Calendar,* and *Trash Panda Haiku* in which some of these poems have previously appeared or are forthcoming.

POSTCARDS FROM TEXAS

making the coffee
truck-stop strong
new school year

cicada song all gone
one air conditioner still drones
before dawn

autumn equinox
still brushing sand
from my earfolds

first cold morning
every dog
a puppy again

gleaners
collect abandoned bedding—
condemned apartments

cigarette drag
last gasp of wildflowers
in November wind

Thanksgiving Day
last pequins ripen
along the fence

gray kingbird feasts—
an unseen harvest
among stripped branches

new moon
blood orange juice
between my fingers

late pepper harvest
in a stoneware bowl
Christmas lights

cold snap
dead bumblebee face up
on the windowsill

unseasonably warm—
glimpsing stone Buddhas
behind a privacy fence

Groundhog Day:
bluebonnet roots
beneath brown grass

plastic rose
juts from a scarred oak
Valentine's day

Equinox
the first mosquito
sighting of spring

first bluebonnets
gunshot trauma kit
in my schoolbag

daylight savings time
the wren sings at sunrise
no matter what

blue jays squabble
in the redbud tree
call to morning prayer

mockingbird nest
eggs abandoned
silent spring

rinse cycle
laundry forgotten
in the rain

For Sale sign gone—
around the demolition notice
rain lilies

rent increase
even the sparrows
have moved on

Port Aransas—
mated pair of whooping cranes
wish you were here

cigarette smoke...
afternoon fog
disappears

floodplain
in my neighbor's yard
duck song

giving notice—
the first dandelions
gone to seed

spring thunder
one grackle call
before the storm

wind turbines
still blades at sunrise
wrapped in fog

hazy sunrise
lost dog sign
slick with dew

rainy season
comes and goes—
unfulfilled promises

two women complain
about least-loved chores
warbler song

olive sapling
extends its first branch
ignored phone calls

after a nightmare—
hearing white-winged doves
foreshadow sunrise

seller's market
all the vacant lots
wildflower fields

feral bee hive
the whole earth humming
beneath our feet

first garden harvest
all of the poems
you'll never write

heirloom tomato
grandmother's pincushion
still fresh

where the prickly pear
became compost—
sunflowers

our path—
tunnel of sunflowers
chorus of honeybees

pulling sticker burrs
from pant legs
one by one

sunflowers
the last silhouette
of sunset

high noon:
homeless hands in trash cans
turkey vultures

a sparrow carcass
almost picked clean—
heat advisory

I want you—
a great blue heron
snags a fish

ruby-throated hummingbird
—for a moment, motionless—
shift in the wind

hot day
ice in the cooler bloodies
my knuckles

skyline trail
our last beer
already warm

heavy gray clouds
move in the wrong direction—
our wilting gardens

eastern swallowtail
the size of my palm
lifelines

summer solstice
waiting for your temper
to subside

heat shimmer
in an unmowed lawn
grass going to seed

wild roses—
all the names
I do not know

century blossoms
tangled in power lines...
moving day

ABOUT THE AUTHOR

Allyson Whipple is the creator of *The Culinary Saijiki*, a blog and podcast project that explores the intersection of food, haiku, and the seasons. She has also authored two chapbooks of free verse poetry: *Come into the World Like That* (2016) and *We're Smaller Than We Think We Are* (2013). During the years she lived in Texas, Allyson served as the board president of *Borderlands: Texas Poetry Review* and co-edited four editions of the *Texas Poetry Calendar*. She now makes her home in St. Louis, Missouri.

www.ingramcontent.com/pod-product-compliance
Lightning Source LLC
Chambersburg PA
CBHW061740070526
44585CB00024B/2758